Eddie tries to reach the cupcakes, but breaks his mother's bowl instead.

Reading Vocabulary Words

disappointed	*notice*
heavier	

High-Frequency Words

fix	*bowl*
smile	*spread*
salad	*pieces*
blue	*kitchen*

Building Future Vocabulary

* These vocabulary words do not appear in this text. They are provided to develop related oral vocabulary that first appears in future texts.

Words:	*lesson*	*address*	*sharp*
Levels:	Library	Silver	Silver

Comprehension Strategy

Asking questions to understand key themes

Fluency Skill

Using phrases to build excitement or to add emphasis or drama

Phonics Skill

Identifying and segmenting spoken words into syllables (news-pa-per, yes-ter-day, dis-ap-point-ed)

Reading-Writing Connection

Writing a paragraph

Home Connection

Send home one of the Flying Colors Take-Home books for children to share with their families.

Differentiated Instruction

Before reading the text, query children to discover their level of understanding of the comprehension strategy — Asking questions to understand key themes. As you work together, provide additional support to children who show a beginning mastery of the strategy.

Focus on ELL

- Introduce the difference between heavy and light.

- Display a book and pencil. Say *The book is heavier than the pencil.* Have children create their own sentences describing classroom objects.

Using This Teaching Version

1. Before Reading

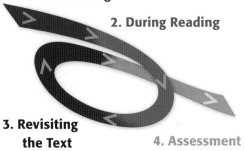

2. During Reading

3. Revisiting the Text

4. Assessment

This Teaching Version will assist you in directing children through the process of reading.

1. **Begin with Before Reading** to familiarize children with the book's content. Select the skills and strategies that meet the needs of your children.

2. **Next, go to During Reading** to help children become familiar with the text, and then to read individually on their own.

3. **Then, go back to Revisiting the Text** and select those specific activities that meet children's needs.

4. **Finally, finish with Assessment** to confirm children are ready to move forward to the next text.

Building Background

- Write the word *notice* on the board. Read it aloud. Ask children what it means to notice something. Ask *Can you think of another definition for notice?* (an announcement in the newspaper)

- Introduce the book by reading the title, talking about the cover illustration, and sharing the overview.

Building Future Vocabulary
Use Interactive Modeling Card: Word Meaning Builder

- Introduce the word *sharp*. Ask children to list any ideas they associate with the word *sharp*. Write these on the Word Meaning Builder.

- Have children list synonyms for *sharp* and then list antonyms.

Introduction to Reading Vocabulary

- On blank cards write: *disappointed*, *notice*, and *heavier*. Read them aloud. Tell children these words will appear in the text of *Cupcakes*.

- Use each word in a sentence for understanding.

Introduction to Comprehension Strategy

- Explain that most stories have a key theme or lesson. Say *Sometimes the key theme is obvious. Other times you must ask questions or keep reading to figure out the theme.*

- Tell children they will be identifying the problem and solution in *Cupcakes*. This information will help them determine the story's theme.

- Using the cover illustration, ask children if they can predict the story's key theme. (no, not enough information)

Introduction to Phonics

- List on the board: **newspaper**. Read the word aloud and use it in a sentence. Say the syllables one at a time.

- Say *Many words can be broken down into parts that are complete words themselves.* Have children locate the word **cupcakes** on the cover and say each part. (**cup**, **cakes**)

- Have children look for other words that can be broken into parts as they read *Cupcakes*.

Modeling Fluency

- Read aloud the first two paragraphs on page 6, modeling how to build excitement or drama as you move from sentence to sentence, emphasizing words and phrases.

- Talk about reading for drama. Explain that we create drama not only with our tone of voice, but with the speed at which we read aloud, and by using pauses effectively.

2 During Reading

Book Talk
Beginning on page T4, use the During Reading notes on the left-hand side to engage children in a book talk. On page 16, follow with Individual Reading.

Book Talk

- Say *The problem the main character deals with is usually the theme. A story may have more than one theme, but the most important is the key theme.*

- **Comprehension Strategy**
  Ask *Who do you think are the story's two main characters?* (a boy, a woman) *What food do you think will be important in the story?* (cupcakes) *How do you know?* (from the title and picture)

Turn to page 2 – Book Talk

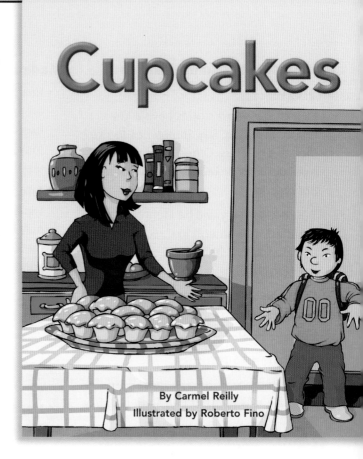

Cupcakes

By Carmel Reilly
Illustrated by Roberto Fino

Cupcakes

By Carmel Reilly

Illustrated by Roberto Fino

Future Vocabulary

- Look at the cover illustration. Say *Mom has been baking. What kinds of things might people use while they are baking?* (stove, bowls, spoons, mixer) Say *Some people bake cupcakes or muffins with fruit. When they bake apple cupcakes, they use a sharp knife to cut the apple.*

- Discuss how to handle sharp items, such as scissors and pencils, safely.

Now revisit pages 4–5

Book Talk

- Ask *What does Eddie notice on the table?* (cupcakes) *Does Eddie like cupcakes?* (yes) *How do you know?* (He is smiling and looking at them.)

- Tell children that Mom will not let Eddie eat more than one cupcake, and Eddie is disappointed. Ask *What kinds of things might disappoint you?*

- **Phonics Skill** Have children locate the word *cupcakes* in the first sentence. Show how to break this word up into syllables. *(cup, cakes)*

Turn to page 4 – Book Talk

Chapter 1 Just One More

Eddie came home from school one afternoon and saw the most beautiful cupcakes on a plate on the kitchen table. They were huge and had thick pink icing.

"Would you like one?" asked Mom.

"Yes, please," replied Eddie.

He picked the biggest cupcake he could see and took a bite.

"These are delicious, Mom," he said.

"That's good," said Mom. "I made them for Grandpa. I'm going to put the rest away now and take them over to him tomorrow."

"All right," said Eddie, but he was a little disappointed because he would have liked another one.

2

Future Vocabulary

- Say *Look at the clock on the wall. What time is it?* (3:30 P.M.) *We can also say it is 3:30 sharp. When we say this,* sharp *means the exact time.*

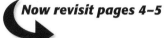

Now revisit pages 4–5

During Reading

Book Talk

- Have children locate the word *notice*. Ask *What does it mean to notice something?* (to see it) *What do you think Eddie notices about the cupcakes in the illustration on page 5?* (The cupcakes are in a box, or tin, on the shelf. Eddie can tell because there is a picture on the box.)

- **Comprehension Strategy** Ask *What do you think Eddie will do?* (try to get the cupcakes) *Do you think he should do this?* (No, his mother told him he could have only one.) *What do you think the story's key theme might be?* (not doing the right thing, disobeying a parent)

Turn to page 6 – Book Talk

Eddie's mom put the cupcakes in a tin and put the tin on a shelf in the kitchen. Then she went out to the garden to pick some lettuce for dinner.

While his mom was outside, Eddie looked up at the tin. There were plenty of cupcakes, he thought.

He was sure his mom wouldn't notice if he took just one more. It would be easy to reach the tin if he stood on a chair.

4

Future Vocabulary

- Say *Things that come to a point are often sharp. What things in this picture might have sharp parts?* (blender blade, edge of counter or shelf, fence)

- Ask *What other sorts of things are sharp?* (knives, tools, swords, pins, needles, claws) *What happens when you touch something sharp?* (You could get hurt.)

Now revisit pages 6–7

Book Talk

- **Fluency Skill** Have children read the second and third paragraphs aloud, using the words and their voice to build excitement and drama.

- Have children find the word *heavier*. Ask *What was heavier than Eddie expected?* (the tin of cupcakes) *Why would a heavy tin be likely to bump into something?* (It was harder to control; Eddie had to wiggle and tug on it to move it to the edge of the shelf.)

- **Phonics Skill** Have children locate the words *newspaper* and *something*. Demonstrate how to say these words one syllable at a time. Have volunteers repeat after you.

Turn to page 8 – Book Talk

Eddie reached up high. He could just feel the bottom of the tin. He tried to pull it to the edge of the shelf, but it was heavier than he thought.

He felt it bump into something. Then he saw his mom's best blue bowl begin to wobble. It was next to the tin and was just about to fall.

Eddie tried to catch it, but he was too late. The bowl fell to the floor and broke into three big pieces.

Eddie looked out the window and saw that his mom was still in the garden.

He quickly picked up the pieces, put them into the trash, and spread newspaper over them, hoping that his mom would not see.

6

Future Vocabulary

- Ask children to look at page 7. Ask *What is on the floor?* (pieces of broken bowl) *Are the pieces likely to be sharp?* (yes)

- Ask *What lesson do you think Eddie will learn in this story?* (not to lie) *Have you learned any lessons when you did something wrong?*

Now revisit pages 8–9

During Reading

Book Talk

- **Comprehension Strategy** Ask *What has Eddie done wrong?* (disobeyed Mom, broken the bowl, and lied about knowing where the bowl is) *Name three possible themes of this story.* (disobeying, breaking something, lying) *Which do you think is the most important?*

➤ Turn to page 10 – Book Talk

2 The Blue Bowl

Just before dinner, Eddie was doing his homework on the kitchen table. His mom was making a salad with the lettuce she had picked from the garden.

She said, "Eddie, have you seen my blue bowl? I want to put the salad into it."

"No, Mom," said Eddie.

8

"That's strange," said Mom, "I'm sure it was there on the shelf. I wonder where I could have put it. Perhaps I left it at Grandpa's house yesterday."

Eddie didn't say anything.

9

Future Vocabulary

- Ask *What is Mom using to cut the lettuce?* (a knife) *Do you think the knife is sharp?* (yes)

- Say *Mom addresses Eddie when she asks him if he knows where her bowl is.* Remind children that *address* can also mean to talk to a group of people. Ask children when or where people might give speeches. (in an auditorium, on television, when participating in an election, at a school assembly) Ask *What does the phrase* address the crowd *mean?* (to talk to the crowd)

Now revisit pages 10–11

During Reading

Book Talk

- Ask *What does Mom notice in the garbage?* (newspaper) *What does she find under it?* (her broken bowl) *Which is heavier, the whole bowl or one of the pieces?* (the whole bowl)

- **Fluency Skill** Have children read page 11 aloud, using the words and their voice to build excitement and drama.

- **Comprehension Strategy** Ask *What questions do you have at this point in the story? What do you think will happen?*

Turn to page 12 – Book Talk

After dinner, Eddie helped his mom clean up, and then he went to his room.

His mom picked up some pieces of paper from the kitchen floor. When she started to put them in the trash, she saw the newspaper.

10

10

Then she noticed something blue underneath the newspaper. She lifted the paper and gasped. There was her best bowl. She picked the pieces out of the trash.

11

Future Vocabulary

• Ask *Is Eddie studying his lessons? Who assigns lessons?* (teachers) *Why must students complete lessons?* (to learn)

Now revisit pages 12–13

During Reading

Book Talk

- Have children read the chapter title. Then ask *How do you think Mom feels?* (unhappy, disappointed) *How can you tell?* (Her arms are crossed, and she is looking down at Eddie.) *How do you think Eddie feels?* (worried, embarrassed) *How can you tell?* (His head is lowered, and he is looking at the floor.) *What do you think will happen to Eddie?*

Turn to page 14 — Book Talk

Chapter 3

Eddie Tells Mom

"Eddie," called Mom.

Eddie walked into the kitchen.

"Yes, Mom?" he said.

Then he saw his mom's face. She looked upset, and Eddie knew right away that she had found the bowl.

"Did you do this?" she asked, pointing to the pieces of bowl on the table.

"Yes," he replied.

"What happened?" she asked. "Why didn't you tell me?"

"I didn't tell you because I was trying to get another cupcake. I was reaching up to get the tin, and I knocked the bowl off the shelf," said Eddie. "I didn't want you to know. I was afraid you would be angry."

12

Future Vocabulary

- Point to the postcards on the wall behind Mom. Ask *What do you put on a postcard to make sure it reaches the right person?* (an address)

- Ask *What information should be included in an address?* (name, street number, street, name of city, state, zip code)

- Ask *What kind of address do people use if they have a computer?* (an e-mail address)

Now revisit pages 14–15

Book Talk

- Have children find the word *disappointed* in the second line on page 14. Ask *Who is disappointed?* (Mom) *Why do you think so?* (because Eddie broke the bowl and didn't tell her)

- **Comprehension Strategy**
Read this page to children. Ask *What questions can you ask yourself to figure out the key theme?* (Why did Eddie lie to Mom? Why was Mom so disappointed?)

Turn to page 16 – Book Talk

"Oh, dear," said Eddie's mom.

She looked very disappointed.

"You're right. I am upset that you broke my best bowl. It's dangerous to try to lift things off that high shelf. You could have really hurt yourself. But the worst thing is that you tried to hide it from me."

14

Eddie felt terrible.

"I know, Mom," he said. "I'm sorry."

"You have to promise me that you won't do anything like this again," said Mom.

"I promise," said Eddie.

15

Future Vocabulary

- **Comprehension Strategy**
  Ask *What lessons has Eddie learned?* (not to disobey, not to break things, not to lie) *Can these lessons be called the themes of a story?* (yes)

- Say *Look at Mom. She's dressed nicely. Some people might say she looks sharp.* Explain that the word *sharp* can be used to describe a person's appearance.

- Say *The word* sharp *can also describe someone who can solve problems quickly or easily.*

Go to page T5 –
Revisiting the Text

During Reading

Book Talk

- Leave this page for children to discover on their own when they read the book individually.

Individual Reading

Have each child read the entire book at his or her own pace while remaining in the group.

Go to page T5 —
Revisiting the Text

Mom gave Eddie a small smile.

"You know, I think I can fix that bowl," she said.

"Do you want me to help you?" asked Eddie.

Eddie's mom gave him a big hug.

"Yes," she replied. "I'd love for you to help me."

16

During independent work time, children can read the online book at:
www.rigbyflyingcolors.com

16

Revisiting the Text

Future Vocabulary
- Use the notes on the right-hand pages to develop oral vocabulary that goes beyond the text. These vocabulary words first appear in future texts. These words are: *lesson*, *address*, and *sharp*.

   Turn back to page 1

Reading Vocabulary Review
Activity Sheet: Clues to Use

- Write these words on the board: *heavier*, *disappointed*, and *notice*. Have volunteers read the words aloud and then use them in a sentence.

- Tell children to find these words in the story and tell what they mean by the way they are used. Allow them to work with a partner to complete the Activity Sheet.

Comprehension Strategy Review
Use Interactive Modeling Card: Main Idea and Supporting Details

- Discuss *Cupcakes*. Have children identify one main idea from this story.

- Tell children they can find details in the text that can support this main idea. Have them list four details and write them in the table legs.

Phonics Review
- Write words from the story on the board: *afternoon, newspaper, something, cupcake, anything, upset, homework,* and *yourself.*

- Read the words aloud and then ask children to break each word down into parts, or syllables.

Fluency Review
- Turn to page 12, partner children, and have them take turns reading the dialogue between Mom and Eddie.

- Remind them how to use their tone of voice, their reading speed, and pauses to build drama or excitement. Explain how emphasizing certain words can add to the listener's enjoyment of the story.

Reading-Writing Connection
Activity Sheet: Story Map

To assist children with linking reading and writing:
- Discuss how to complete the Story Map for *Cupcakes*.

- Have children use the Story Map to plan their own fictional story. Have them write the first paragraph of their story.

Assessing Future Vocabulary

Work with each child individually. Ask questions that elicit each child's understanding of the Future Vocabulary words. Note each child's responses:

- What lessons have you learned in class? What lessons have you learned playing with your friends?
- Have you ever had to address a large group of people?
- What does it mean to say a knife is sharp? What does it mean to say someone looks sharp?

Assessing Comprehension Strategy

Work with each child individually. Note each child's understanding of asking questions to understand key themes:

- Who are the characters in *Cupcakes*?
- Did Eddie do anything wrong?
- What should Eddie have done instead?
- What do you think is the key theme of this story?
- What helps you identify a story's key theme?

Assessing Phonics

Work with each child individually. Note each child's responses for understanding how to segment words into syllables:

- Use these words: *beautiful*, *easy*, *tomorrow*, *another*, *plenty*, and *heavier*.
- Say a word and have each child repeat the word one syllable at a time.
- Did each child understand how to segment the words?
- Did each child correctly segment the words into syllables? Did he or she include all the syllables?

Assessing Fluency

Have each child read page 6 to you. Note each child's understanding of using phrases to build excitement or to add emphasis or drama:

- Was each child able to vary speed and tone of voice when reading this page?
- Was each child able to emphasize certain words to help build excitement or drama?
- Was each child able to use pauses for dramatic effect?

Interactive Modeling Cards

Word Meaning Builder

New Word	Ideas	Synonyms	Antonyms
sharp	feeling, texture	pointed, spiked, thorny	full, rounded, flat, blunt

Directions: With children, fill in the Word Meaning Builder using the word *sharp*.

Main Idea and Supporting Details

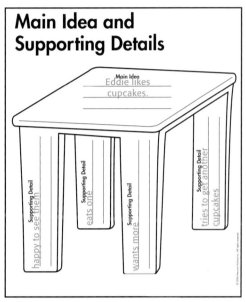

Main Idea
Eddie likes cupcakes.

Supporting Detail
happy to see them

Supporting Detail
eats one

Supporting Detail
wants more

Supporting Detail
tries to get another cupcakes

Directions: With children, fill in the Main Idea and Supporting Details for *Cupcakes*.

Discussion Questions

- What did Eddie want in this book? (Literal)
- When Eddie hid the pieces of the broken bowl, did that solve his problem? (Critical Thinking)
- How do you think Eddie felt when Mom discovered the broken bowl? (Inferential)

Activity Sheets

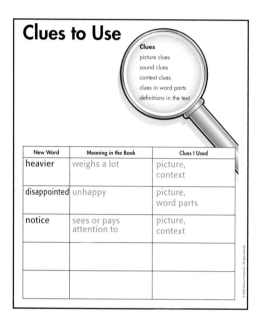

Clues to Use

New Word	Meaning in the Book	Clues I Used
heavier	weighs a lot	picture, context
disappointed	unhappy	picture, word parts
notice	sees or pays attention to	picture, context

Clues
picture clues
sound clues
context clues
clues in word parts
definitions in the text

Directions: Have children fill in the Clues to Use for the words *heavier*, *disappointed*, and *notice*.

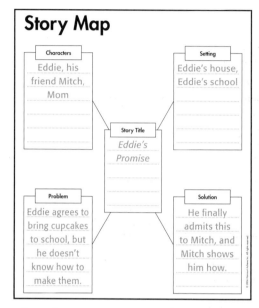

Story Map

Characters
Eddie, his friend Mitch, Mom

Setting
Eddie's house, Eddie's school

Story Title
Eddie's Promise

Problem
Eddie agrees to bring cupcakes to school, but he doesn't know how to make them.

Solution
He finally admits this to Mitch, and Mitch shows him how.

Directions: Have children use the Story Map to outline another story about Eddie and the cupcakes. Ask them to write the first paragraph of the story.
Optional: Have children complete their story.